THE WHITEWATER KAYAKER'S LITTLE BOOK OF WISDOM

Written by Corran Addison

ICS BOOKS, Inc.
Merrillville, IN

Thanks to:

Dad for getting me my first kayak....
Mum for letting me go....
Richard Pocock for making me get up at 4 a.m. all the time....
Jerome Truran and Richard Fox for really teaching me how to kayak....
Norbert Sattler for coaching me to the Olympics....
Christine Degremont for paying my way to the Olympics....
Rusty for being the best friend a man can have....
Riot Kayaks for giving me the time to write this....
And
all those that have been on all the crazy river trips over the years.

Introduction

Corran Addison was born in South Africa, where he first got in a kayak at the age of 6. Since his auspicious start, he has become one of the leading figures in whitewater kayaking, and definitely the most controversial. His paddling career spans more than 20 years, 6 continents, 5 disciplines and 2 lives. He is the world record holder for the highest waterfall ever run in a kayak (100 f.t vertical), has the world speed/vertical waterfall record (25 m in 57 seconds), has numerous first descents and records world wide, competed in the 1992 Barcelona Olympic games, is a many time U.S., European and South African freestyle champion, and is the 1995 World Freestyle Championship silver medalist.

Corran has been responsible for designing some of the worlds best-selling and most innovative kayaks. His equipment and technical achievements over the last decade, and his regular articles and films in media circles, have significantly aided in the rapid advancement of the sport of whitewater kayaking into mainstream acceptance. His last swim from his kayak was in Southern France on the Verdon in 1986, where he nearly drowned trying to save a friend. He is a true believer in CPR, and is a wilderness EMT. Corran is the master instructor for the United States West Coast division of the World Kayak Federation, is a ski and snowboard instructor, snowboard patroller, and avid inline skater and mountain biker. He co-owns Rip International and Riot Kayaks.

1. Kayaking is as safe as you want it to be.

2. A bad day on the river is better than a good day at work.

3. It's only water. When everything goes to hell, keep things in perspective.

4. All your constitutional rights are lost once you enter the rapid.

5. "When you scout a rapid from the bank, you have to remember that when you are in your boat, all you can see is a horizon line...and spray...."

—Dan Gavere 1995 Europa Cup Freestyle Champion.

6. When you're in a foreign country and someone has to accompany the boats on land while the team flies, volunteer. You'll have many experiences to remember.

7. Every expedition has a leader and a gofer. Befriend the gofer.

8. As amusing as it is to watch your kayaks flying across the intersection, it's safer to check the tie job regularly.

9. Never paddle on flooded rivers. All kinds of debris is coming down, and trees are a real concern.

10. Paddling flooded rivers is the ultimate rush. Use extreme caution.

11. You can only have so much technique. After that you just have to pull harder.

12. If you do what you have always done, then you are not learning anything.

13. Take photos of the silly moments. These make the best memories.

14. The river can be your most comforting companion.

15. The river is a powerful ally.

16. The river could be your most deadly enemy.

17. Every time you leave the lights on, they build another dam and a river dies.

18. Pee in the water, not on the bank. It has a less adverse effect on the habitat.

19. Go out of your way to learn all you can about your sport.

20. Offer advice to others without them having to ask for it, but don't force it on them.

21. Kids are immortal. Adults are not.

22. Kids are fearless. The rest of us remember negative past experiences.

23. Allow your children to find their own paddling path.

24. If you have a good product idea, think before you make somebody else rich off it.

25. Share your ideas with the rest of the paddling world so that they too may benefit from your intellect and experience.

26. Don't be afraid to chuck everything and go on an extended paddling vacation. You can always restart.

27. A river trip, like success or life, is a journey, not a destination.

28. If you have more money than time, our priorities are backward.

29. You can be competitive with your friends, but keep it in perspective.

30. Demand the best from yourself, and accept nothing less.

31. Never paddle alone.

32. When in doubt...scout.

33. The price you pay for a helmet is directly related to what you think your head is worth.

34. Sometimes you need to break the rules and paddle alone.

35. Join the World Kayak Federation. Give back to the sport that brings you so much.

36. Training at 5 a.m. in sub-zero temperatures is character building.

37. Offer to take a photo of the trip photographer. After all, he went everywhere you did.

38. Always do a mental roll call in the same order. It's easier to notice a missing person in a large group.

39. There is no one tool for every job. The same applies to kayak designs.

40. Always consider the consequences of your actions.

41. "There is nothing quite so fun as simply messing about in boats"

—Unknown

42. Paddle every rapid as if it were the last.

43. "You know, sometimes I think that people are too serious."

—Norbert Sattler 1972
Olympic Kayak Silver Medalist

44. Everyone needs to get stranded in a cold canyon in the middle of the night with no food or water. Yeah, right.

45. If it happens a second time, you're not thinking.

46. Buy a paddle bag. It'll protect your equipment from damage, and the airlines are more likely to replace your paddle should anything happen.

47. My worst days are more exciting than most peoples best. That choice is also yours.

48. Try a K1 sprint kayak with a wing paddle. Be prepared to swim.

49. The joy of paddling a new boat lasts only as long as the boat looks new. Look after your equipment, and the pleasure will last.

50. The forward stroke is the most important technique of all and the most neglected.

51. Always use a layering system in variable weather conditions.

52. Get a laptop computer and an internet server. You can access any information about the country or river you are in from anywhere in the world.

53. Try to paddle with people who are better than you.

54. If you are the best in your area, then paddle with someone who's goal is to be better than you.

55. Sometimes you must paddle for yourself. Know these days.

56. Sometimes you must paddle for companionship. Realize this at the outset.

57. Compliment an inferior paddler on their efforts.

58. Date a masseuse. You're a sportsman, right?

59. Give back to the river more than you take from it so that your children may too enjoy it.

60. Watch the video "Fast and Clean."

61. "When I look at a rapid, I try to assess the state that I will be in when I get to the bottom. If it is not a state that I approve of, then I won't run it."

—John Wassen, kayak legend

62. Most kayaks are trimmed with the seat too far back. Don't be shy about moving the seat forward so that the kayak sits in the water with the bow slightly down. A low stern makes them slow and sluggish.

63. Take kayaking lessons from a reputable WKF certified school. You'll improve much faster.

64. A little fear is a good thing. Paralysis is not.

65. "I felt unwell."
—Stan Rickets on the effects of getting thoroughly trashed in a large hole.

66. It is better to be in your boat and mostly out of control, than out of your boat and completely out of control.

67. In your kayak, there is always the faint hope of recovery. Out of it, you are at the mercy of the river.

68. The best way to make a living is by doing something you love for money.

69. When you make a living from your hobby, it ceases to be a hobby. Remember why you started.

70. Take your boat out at least once in sub-zero conditions. You'll appreciate the spring runoff.

71. Ever heard of Giles Zoc?

72. Do you know who Ziggi Horn is?

73. Find out about the pioneers who made this sport great.

74. Watch a kayak and a surfing video back-to-back. Look for inspiration.

75. If you believe that you are the best, then you are halfway there.

76. Don't be too eager in encouraging others to learn how to kayak. If everyone paddled the rivers, they would be crowded.

77. Shoulder injuries are the most common. Never extend your hands behind you.

78. When buying a kayak, listen to your friends' advice, but take their ability and exposure to the latest innovations into account.

79. Always check your equipment for wear or failure.

80. There is nothing more irritating or dangerous than an intermediate who thinks he's an expert. Know your ability.

81. Remember why you started kayaking. It's not to prove yourself, but to amuse yourself.

82. Paddling on your home river is fun, but there is nothing like an adventure.

83. A corollary to Murphy's Law: The possibility of something going wrong is directly proportionate to the probability of it going wrong.

84. Addison's Law: On an expedition, everything will go wrong.

85. Adrenaline is the greatest drug of all. Administer as needed.

86. If you make the same mistake twice, you're not thinking.

87. You learn from your mistakes. Make lots of them.

88. Take a non-paddler on a kayak trip for a date. It'll be the best they've ever had.

89. Clean up the camp sites left by others so that next time you are there, the river is the way it was supposed to be.

90. An Eskimo role is not a polar bear sandwich.

91. Fear breeds respect.

92. Play truant from work once a year and go kayaking.

93. It's better to ask for forgiveness than to ask for permission.

94. Pick your fights well. You can't win every race.

95. Americans have bad reputations as tourists. Go out of your way to dispel this unfortunate rumor. Be extra friendly.

96. It doesn't matter how many carbohydrates are in a beer. It's not a suitable breakfast for a day on the river.

97. If you are poor, you can't afford to replace second-rate equipment, so buy only the best money can get.

98. The way to run a hard rapid is to look for the easy line.

99. When you've had the best day you've ever had, remember that one day you'll have an even better one.

100. If everything runs smoothly, then it's not an adventure.

101. When you are in Nepal, and your boats are in Bali, then it's an expedition.

102. The greatest feeling is when you're so scared you can hardly move, and then you get the courage to go for it.

103. If you use drugs, then you'll only every be second best.

104. Invite some friends over and watch the films "Deliverance," "The Trap," "Whitewater Rebels," and "The Endless Summer."

105. Try to bring your own firewood on overnight trips. Burning driftwood adversely affects the delicate ecosystem.

106. Encourage your local university and high schools to start a whitewater program.

Better to walk than swim.

107. Walk rapids you are not comfortable with. Ultimately the river must win in order to keep the challenge alive.

108. If you want to kayak for a living, don't expect to make a fortune.

109. If you kayak for a living, a single digit annual income is a fortune.

110. Being happy is more important than anything.

111. It takes years of dedication to be the best. Don't give up.

112. Paddle a river simply for its beauty.

113. "I don't want to talk to you anymore about my short paddle. I love my paddle."

—1995 World Championship finalist
Nico Chassing on his
177 cm freestyle paddle.

114. Your body is a temple. Treat it as such.

115. Before scoffing at an equipment innovation, try to see what the inventor was thinking. He was sure of his convictions.

116. Don't rely on your skills. Have a back-up plan.

117. Most backup plans don't work, so rely on your skills and judgement.

118. "When racing stops being fun, I'll stop racing."

—John Lugbill, Five-time World Whitewater Champion.

119. Just when things can't get worse on an expedition, believe me. They will.

120. After things get worse, it'll become a disaster.

121. The definition of a successful expedition is: a disaster you wouldn't have missed for anything in the world.

122. There is nothing wrong with "Kodak courage."

123. Don't get killed over a photo. Your mother prefers the real thing.

124. Analyze everything to the max. Devise solutions for each situation, and perfect them.

125. If you are married and you kayak, there is a conflict of interest. Balance your time carefully, and you can have your cake and eat it too.

126. Try not to move dead trees or wood. Termite cultures are at work and are part of the delicate ecosystem.

127. Beware which hand signals you use abroad. Some inconspicuous U.S. signals are very offensive in other countries.

128. Take a logger boating. Show him the benefits to the alternate use for trees.

129. Question what an instructor tells you. You'll learn more, and he might too.

130. It's better to be portaging a rapid and be wishing that you had run it, than to be running it and wishing that you had portaged.

131. "I look at all the cool things that people are doing now, and I think maybe we did know what we were doing back then."

—Bob McDougal,
original extreme kayaker

132. Rent an old mold, and make yourself a fiberglass kayak. It's inexpensive to make, and you'll learn a lot.

133. Working with fiberglass is the most irritating, frustrating thing. After one kayak, you'll gladly pay retail for the next.

134. Don't confuse kayaking with religion. It's not one.

135. A perfect surf can be a religious experience.

136. Excellence. Perfection. Getting there is half the fun.

137. Every kayaker should run the Grand Canyon once.

138. Push yourself physically. You get out what you put in.

139. If you think your paddle is great, try a carbon bent-shaft 25 oz. paddle. Yours will be up for sale.

140. Peer pressure can push your limits, but there is a time and a place for it.

141. If you are having more fun than someone else, don't rub it in. Take them with you.

142. Make an effort to communicate in the language of the people whose country you are kayaking in, and the world will be offered to you.

143. Just because you are an American abroad, doesn't mean you have to act like one. Dispel the myth.

144. *Avec la langue on peut aller jusqu' a Rome.*

145. You know when you lean back in a chair too far and you suddenly catch yourself before you almost fall. That's how kayaking should feel.

146. I've been working on my forward stroke for 20 years, and it's still not perfect. Don't kid yourself. Practice, practice, practice.

147. The feeling of a warm body next to you after a long day in cold water makes teaching your spouse to kayak worth the time.

148. Remember this acronym. MICK for Minimum Impact Camp Kayaking.

149. Some of my best lessons came from beginners. Be open to anyone's suggestions and ideas.

150. Don't just sit and watch the worst happen. The least you can do is help it happen.

151. Ask for a discount. If you don't ask, you won't get one.

152. Don't name your firstborn after your favorite river. That might change.

153. Don't name your firstborn after your favorite kayaker either.

154. Second place is the first loser. Good Grief!

155. Ask a girl you meet in a bar if she likes hiking alone. Have her run shuttle so you can paddle alone. No - learn to Hitchhike.

156. Injuries happen. Nurse them, but don't dwell on them.

157. The most expensive violins are the most delicate, and require the greatest care. The same applies to kayak equipment.

158. If your equipment manufacturer tells you not to alter anything, pay heed. They built it, so they should know.

159. Sometimes equipment isn't as well built as it could be, so your changes might be good. Think it over carefully.

160. "The best freestyle kayaking is 60% water, 30% air and 10% rock."

—Karl Gustavsen

161. Paddle a canoe once. It's really hard and fun. At worst you'll appreciate kayaking.

162. True adventure is when you have to break the ice off your wet suit in the morning.

163. If you have to pop your ears in the middle of a drop, chances are it's way too big.

164. We all have dreams. Make one of yours to be the best paddler you can be.

165. There is no feeling more romantic than sitting beside a river with a special person after an exciting day, and watching the sun set together. Try this.

166. If human waste cannot be removed, designate a camp latrine and bury it in one place at least 2 feet deep. 50 ft away from a H_2O source

167. Your kids will always learn faster than you. Get used to it.

168. Everybody swims eventually.

169. Make friends with a rafter. They can carry a lot of stuff on overnight trips.

170. Be a good winner and a better loser. You'll get respect for it.

171. Next time win! You'll command even more respect.

172. The best equipment won't make you the best paddler, but it sure makes the journey easier and more enjoyable.

173. Tell someone where you are going and when you'll be back. Allow for the inevitable delays.

174. You never know who you are going to meet on the river, so always pack extra beer.

175. I love to say, "I'll worry about it when I get there". Usually I end up worrying.

176. Try paddling a C1. It's really hard, and extremely fun.

177. If someone tells you that it can't be done, what they are saying is that they can't do it.

178. Do an overnight trip. Watch the river run into the sunset.

179. You'll only underdress for conditions once.

180. Own a piece of junk so that others will volunteer to drive.

181. Don't use antiquated gear. New technology is worth its weight in gold.

182. More kayakers die on the road than on the river. Remember that.

183. You can never have too much beer on the Grand Canyon.

184. The two most important people on an expedition are a mechanic and an EMT.

185. If that is not possible, then bring along a translator.

186. Know at least one good camp fire story. Learn to tell it well.

187. I've slipped and swum many rapids I wouldn't run in my kayak. Scout and portage with care.

188. If you are the best, you won't be for long. There is always someone who learns faster, and trains harder.

189. "My speciality is being right when others are wrong."

—Winston Churchill

190. Take your boss and his family rafting. Guide the boat yourself and show them a good time. It's a cheap trick, but it works.

191. If you are a lousy guide, take his main competitor rafting instead.

192. Use environmentally friendly soaps on river trips. Don't wash in the river + don't dump wash water there either.

193. Use sand to wash dishes, not soap.

194. Always double pass a trucker's hitch, especially on other peoples' ropes.

195. If you kayak within your limits, it's safer than taking a bath.

196. The Russians use pig bladders wrapped in canvas, framed with saplings cut at the put-in, and cork for life vests. Be thankful for free enterprise next time you complain about the cost of equipment.

197. Take time to smell the roses.

198. Race your own race, but pay attention to the other competitors.

199. Give blood to the Red Cross. You might need it one day.

200. Eat before you paddle and directly afterward. Especially on multi-day trips.

201. You might be tough, but a short sleeve paddle jacket in snow conditions is just plain dumb.

202. Wash your capalene regularly. No one wants to run shuttle with you if you stink.

203. Don't shout over the river roar. You won't win.

204. Develop and use hand and paddle signals. Use industry standards whenever possible.

205. If a good day seems like it is lasting forever, drag it out some more.

206. Take an intimate partner on an expedition. By its end you will either be inseparable, or not on speaking terms.

207. Always take a spare spray skirt. You can survive without everything else but this.

208. Learn to brace effectively. It's better than a role.

209. Apply the lessons you learn in your boat to life.

210. Apply the lessons you learn in life to your boating.

211. On Jacky Joyner Kersey: "The great emotion shared by this husband and wife team is the very definition of sporting companionship."

212. The best paddlers are often the worst instructors.

213. “It’s fun being scared, but not so scared that I can’t move.”

—Bernd Sommer, 1996 Pre-world Championship silver medalist

214. Look both ways before crossing the street.

215. Giles Zoc was the first person ever to win five world championships in whitewater.

216. Don't stand on the top rung of a ladder.

217. Never put a knife in a toaster.

218. Life has its risks. Kayaking is one of them. Use common sense, and there is never reason to fear.

219. Just because you stop paddling, does not make the river stop moving. Keep going!

220. Next time you complain about a cold river swim, think of those who learn to paddle with crocodiles in Africa.

221. Norbert Sattler was doing cartwheels in a 9 lb. slalom boat in the 1970s. Look to the past to understand our sports future.

222. People die. Better in their boats than in a car wreck. Move on and enjoy yourself.

223. Don't smoke on the river. The fumes are offensive to many who are there to enjoy nature.

224. Always carry a power bar. They may taste terrible, but they can be a life saver on a cold river.

225. The harder your skirt is to get on, the better it works.

226. Disregard the difficulty rating system. It's misleading and varies from region to region.

227. "I'll kayak and climb until I drop."
—Royal Robbins, founder
Royal Robins Clothing Company

228. Experience local culture to the max.

229. When flying with a kayak, arrive at the airport 30 minutes earlier than required. It gives airport attendants the time they need to deal with the boat.

230. Arriving early allows you to pick out a friendly looking attendant. More often than not it is up to their discretion whether to check the boat in or not.

231. Wear a buoyancy aid with just enough floatation to keep your unconscious body on the surface, but not so much that it impedes your ability to swim.

232. Know the difference between river right and wave right. Wave right is river left and vice versa.

233. Take a day off paddling, and hike up a river valley you would never paddle down.

234. Lie to everyone else about your abilities, but never yourself.

235. No one respects a liar, so don't get caught.

236. On Lynford Christy: Stand up for your convictions, but know when to stop.

237. Anyone who is scared of kayaking had a bad teacher.

238. There are two kinds of whitewater kayakers:
Fearless ones who have yet to take a beating.
Cautious paddlers who have taken a beating.

239. Sex-on-the-beach is a common thing, but not as a drink in a whitewater environment. Indulge yourself.

240. It's better to take your slammer neat, than on the rocks.

241. Never lend your equipment to others. Always know its exact history for safety reasons.

242. Never rely on your equipment if you don't know its history.

243. If that person you want a date with needs to borrow your stuff, go for it.

244. You cannot escape your problems on the river, but it is a great place to solve them.

245. Start next season's training program the day this season ends. It is easier to maintain a level of fitness than it is to develop one.

246. A Swiss army knife is a must.

247. "I want to be in control all the time. Some people like being out of control, but not me."

—Jan Kellner, 1991 World Freestyle Champion

248. "Sometimes it's fun to be a little out of control in a big hole."

—Bernd Sommer, 1996 Pre-world Freestyle Championship silver medalist

249. Learn to do with your kayak what MacGuyver can do with a paper clip.

250. It's okay to take chances, not risks.

251. Trees are bad news. Stay away from them at all costs.

252. Paddle into a big hole that you are scared of. You will be surprised at how fun it can be (in a twisted sort of way).

253. "Sometimes things just don't go as planned, but you can't lose focus of your goal."

—Richard Fox, Five-time World Kayak Champion

254. Not until you have been on an expedition with them, will you know who, and what your friends really are.

255. Your first instinct is usually the right one.

256. The downstream paddler has the right-of-way. Be courteous.

257. "There is no try. Only do, or do not. If you try, you will fail."

—Yoda, Jedi Master

258. Even in rivalry there is a companionship that ties us together in the same sport.

259. It's better to have the skills to keep you out of trouble, than the skills to get you out of trouble.

260. "It's better to die in your boat than it is to swim." I don't think so!

—Eric Jackson, WKF President

261. Ever tried to ski on ice with rounded edges? Not very effective. The same applies to kayaking. Question all that the industry knows.

262. If at first you don't succeed, cheat.

263. If that doesn't work, lie.

264. When you have finished with those, learn the skills to succeed, and neither will be necessary.

265. Don't buy a kayak that will take care of you, get one that is fun and that will make you learn.

266. The best anti-theft device for a car stereo system is old capalene underwear hanging from the volume knob.

267. Paddle with a portable stereo/radio. Your favorite music will accentuate your favorite play spot.

268. Paddle a 20 lb. carbon kayak for a week, and then try to convince yourself it's not worth the cost.

269. Learn self-rescue. Good paddlers are more likely to take you along when they don't have to chase your stuff if you swim.

270. If in doubt about the quality of water while on an expedition, stay away from ice in your drinks. Freezing doesn't kill germs.

271. We'd still live in caves without duct tape. Always have some handy.

272. Save up for the kayak of your dreams. Most shops will work out a payment program with you.

273. The only use for a river knife is for making PB&J sandwiches.

274. Always carry a throw bag. With luck you'll never need it.

275. Never tie your keys in the boat. You'll always save your skin, but the same cannot be said for the kayak.

276. Ziggi Horn was the first kayaker ever to get an Olympic gold medal—in the 1972 Munich Olympics.

277. You can never teach too many women to paddle. This sport is 90% male dominated.

278. "I ran my best race ever, and Johnson was still faster."

—Carl Lewis

279. A river trip is also a road trip. Expect the adventure to start when you turn the engine on.

280. Drink lots of water. Preventive medicine is better than corrective.

281. To convert cubic feet per second to cubic meters per second, divide by 27.

282. If paddling becomes monotonous, try a new kayak. It's a welcome change.

283. Be tolerant of the reasons others paddle, and how they paddle.

284. Everything is runable. The question rather, is by whom?

285. Don't fight the river. You won't win. Out-think it.

286. If you don't have a good hands role, get a spare paddle.

287. Go on a river trip with strangers. You'll become the best of friends.

288. "If you are broke, borrow $2 from four friends. They'll never ask for it back, and you'll get a meal."
—Lee Bonfigleo, 1993 Freestyle World Championship finalist

289. Dispose of your broken kayak correctly. Most manufacturers have a recycling program.

290. Cross-linked polyethylene is now recyclable. Call you local manufacturer about how to dispose of the plastic correctly.

291. Always tie your kayak on its side or upside down to avoid deformation of the hull.

292. "I don't understand why more women don't paddle. I love getting pounded in big holes."

—Brenda 'Brends daar' Ernst,
U.S. freestyle paddler

293. Use caution if you decide to make a fireside seat from your plastic kayak. Thermoforming plastics like linear polyethylene melt and are also unstable in warm environments.

294. Beware the "Fascination of the abomination!" When everything goes wrong in your boat, do something.

295. Check your drain plug and skirt before every rapid. The last thing you need is extra water on board.

296. Will you look back on your life and say "I did too much," or "I wish I had done more"?

297. Make friends with the farmer who lives on the river. You can get river levels, a shuttle and a place to camp.

298. "Rumors of my death are greatly exaggerated."

—Mark Twain

299. Don't always talk about boating. You'll become a bore.

300. C1 paddlers can be recognized at campsites by the less-than-vertical walking posture and illegal smiles.

301. Just because you're on the wave, doesn't mean you're surfing.

302. Don't live on the edge. Kayak on it.

303. Never leave on a road trip without a copy of *Playboy*. It makes great reading, and it also has unusual articles.

304. Go snorkeling below a rapid that many people swim. You'll be surprised by the treasures that lie below.

305. Do a moonlight run of your favorite river.

306. If you come across a slalom or freestyle paddler doing a workout, ask if you may join in before you get in the way.

307. If you are a serious athlete working out at a popular spot, ask others if they would like to join you, and explain the nature of the workout.

308. An ender is an ender, but does it count if no one sees it?

309. Paddle with a group, but ignore them so that you can be alone.

310. Bring water to a boil makes it safe to drink.--Wilderness Medicine Practice Guidelines

311. Don't pee in your wet suit.

312. Never seal launch a composite kayak.

313. If you have owned a car without rain gutters, then you know what one with is worth.

314. Next time you break a plastic kayak, stop and think about the care David Hearn took on his 9 lb. canoe he used to win the 1985 world championships, and ask yourself if you really were being careful?

315. Freestyle kayaks make lousy creek boats. Decide on your discipline before you buy the latest trend.

316. Ever notice that it is the beginners that have all the latest rescue equipment?

317. When paddling with people below your standards, offer to carry the safety gear.

318. If a swim is likely, use airbags, otherwise discard them. The saved weight is all it might take to avoid a swim.

319. "It's time for another mind game."

—Dennis Rodman Chicago Bulls

320. If you don't have a trip leader, then by the end of the trip you'll have ten. Elect one and respect his decisions.

321. When reserving an airplane ticket, tell the airline that you will be traveling with a kayak, and have confirmation that they will transport it printed on the ticket.

322. It is as exciting to imagine yourself running unrealistic waterfalls and cascades, as it is to actually run the easier ones. Indulge yourself.

323. It is better to regret having done something, than to regret not having done it.

324. It is also better to return another day and succeed, than to try today and fail.

325. Unless you are Richard Fox or Jon Lugbill, you have work to do. Practice.

326. Paddle barefoot and with bare hands. Paddling with shoes and gloves is like taking a shower with a rain coat...!

327. Only your best friends leave their smelly gear, candy wrappers and gas tab for you to deal with.

328. What are friends for?

329. "I want to play the whole river, not just one spot, or one trick".

—Oli Grau, 1995 World Freestyle Champion

330. Go to the bathroom before putting on a one-piece dry suit.

331. Don't exceed your abilities. Be honest with yourself even if you lie to others.

332. Store your kayak in a cool, dry place, hung vertically if possible.

333. Paddle once at sunup. It's worth the early start.

334. Tolerate the paddling priorities of others.

335. Spend a day scouting waterfalls, looking for lines you would never seriously consider running yourself.

336. All manufacturers lie about the weight of their kayaks. If you can't easily lift it, then it is too heavy, regardless of the advertised weight.

337. Plastic is durable, but is non-repairable. Composite can always be fixed. Consider this when buying.

338. Before you buy what the salesman recommends, find out about his paddling abilities and paddling style. It may well conflict with yours.

339. There is no safety substitute for the best equipment money can buy—except knowledge.

340. Never tie a trailing rope onto your kayak that you can't easily release from the most tangled position.

341. The easiest way to recognize a canoeist from a kayaker is buy the size of the life jacket indicating the high swim to paddle ratio. Canoeing is very hard.

342. "I'll never let slalom get in the way of kayaking."

—Eric Jackson, President,
World Kayak Federation

343. Bad outfitting killing you? It might. Get a boat that fits properly so that you don't have to outfit it.

344. When parting on an expedition, don't forget to apply for a visa for every country you will pass into, even those whose borders you will cross by river.

345. Tip the airport porter who is handling your kayak. Ask him to take extra care that it gets onto your flight.

346. Every time you run a rapid, ask yourself if there was a better way to do it.

347. It is good to question yourself, but sometimes just be content to enjoy the moment.

348. Write to your congressman in support of local river or environmental issues.

349. Write to the leaders of other nations in support of their environmental issues and efforts.

350. The owner of a car must always tie the boats on. He knows how he wants it done.

351. Spend the whole day in one spot. You'll learn an amazing amount.

352. Spend an evening watching videos of other extreme sports. Try one of them.

353. Inviter your paddling buddies over for dinner. Talk about something other than kayaking.

354. Teach the neighbor's kid to paddle.

355. Go to the drive on a slow night on a commercial raft bus, and throw a party with the guides.

356. A shop that has 20 boats of the same model isn't necessarily selling the best boat, but possibly the best factory deal they could get. Question motives. Make your own call.

357. A life jacket with too much floatation is just as dangerous as one with too little.

358. Don't forget your take-apart paddle. It's no good to anyone at home.

359. Carry a good first aid kit. There are many designed specifically for this sport.

360. Don't be mislead by market perception of foot brace systems. It's better for the foot brace to break than your ankle.

361. If you are confusing the security loop on your kayak with the pull cord on your skirt, tie a knot or a ball on the skirt for easy recognition while upside down.

362. "You can't give up, because if you give up, well...you've given up."

—Dean Cummins, 1995 World Extreme Ski Champion

363. "I don't know much about gods, but sometimes I think the river is a big, brown god."

—Unknown